Bank Street

ABOUT THE BANK STREET READY-TO-READ SERIES

More than seventy-five years of educational research, innovative teaching, and quality publishing have earned The Bank Street College of Education its reputation as America's most trusted name in early childhood education.

Because no two children are exactly alike in their development, the Bank Street Ready-to-Read series is written on three levels to accommodate the individual stages of reading readiness of children ages three through eight.

○ *Level 1:* **GETTING READY TO READ (Pre-K–Grade 1)**
Level 1 books are perfect for reading aloud with children who are getting ready to read or just starting to read words or phrases. These books feature large type, repetition, and simple sentences.

● *Level 2:* **READING TOGETHER (Grades 1–3)**
These books have slightly smaller type and longer sentences. They are ideal for children beginning to read by themselves who may need help.

○ *Level 3:* **I CAN READ IT MYSELF (Grades 2–3)**
These stories are just right for children who can read independently. They offer more complex and challenging stories and sentences.

All three levels of The Bank Street Ready-to-Read books make it easy to select the books most appropriate for your child's development and enable him or her to grow with the series step by step. The levels purposely overlap to reinforce skills and further encourage reading.

We feel that making reading fun is the single most important thing anyone can do to help children become good readers. We hope you will become part of Bank Street's long tradition of learning through sharing.

The Bank Street College of Education

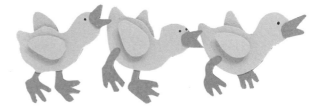

For Julian
—D.O.

To Sam
—J.M.

For a free color catalog describing Gareth Stevens' list of high-quality books and multimedia programs, call 1-800-542-2595 (USA) or 1-800-461-9120 (Canada). Gareth Stevens Publishing's Fax: (414) 225-0377.
See our catalog, too, on the World Wide Web: http://gsinc.com

Library of Congress Cataloging-in-Publication Data

Orgel, Doris.
    Two crows counting / by Doris Orgel ; illustrated by Judith Moffatt.
      p. cm. -- (Bank Street ready-to-read)
    Summary: Two crows, one big and one small, count things they see from one to ten and then back down again.
    ISBN 0-8368-1617-X (lib. bdg.)
    [1. Counting. 2. Crows--Fiction. 3. Stories in rhyme.] I. Moffatt, Judith, ill. II. Title.
III. Series.
PZ8.3.068Tw 1996
[E]--dc20   96-11067

This edition first published in 1996 by
Gareth Stevens Publishing
1555 North RiverCenter Drive, Suite 201
Milwaukee, Wisconsin 53212 USA

Printed in Mexico

1 2 3 4 5 6 7 8 9 99 98 97 96

Bank Street Ready-to-Read™

Two Crows Counting

by Doris Orgel
Illustrated by Judith Moffatt

A Byron Preiss Book

Gareth Stevens Publishing
MILWAUKEE

Big crow, small crow,
on the wing,
counting, counting
everything. . . .

1 ONE sun rising

2 TWO shadows gliding

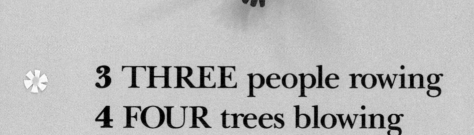

3 THREE people rowing
4 FOUR trees blowing

5 FIVE cats lapping
6 SIX socks flapping

13

14

7 SEVEN herons wading
8 EIGHT geese parading

9 NINE farmers haying
10 TEN children playing.

Small crow, big crow,
home they go,
counting things
they see below. . . .

10 TEN children snoozing
9 NINE farmers snoring

8 EIGHT geese resting
7 SEVEN herons nesting

23

6 SIX socks hardly stirring
5 FIVE cats purring

4 FOUR trees standing
3 THREE boats landing

2 TWO shadows slowing

1 ONE sun glowing.

Big crow, small crow,
dreaming deep,
counting nothing,
fast asleep.